Unlocking Your Financial Potential

Reframing Your Money-Mindset

Kim Aronson

Book edited by S. F. Wilson

Acknowledgements

Thank you to S. F. Wilson for the amazing editing of this book. If you need a reliable editor, you can contact her at sfbk.editing@gmail.com

Thank you, Rosy, for always being willing to point me in the right direction.

Dedication

To my parents Solveig & Thorkild.
You taught me many valuable lessons about money, by not having any.

Epigraph

The privilege of a lifetime is to become who you truly are
- C. G. Jung

Contents

All Wisdom Manuals

All The Books in The Wisdom Manuals series:

The Conscious Caregiver's Compass
- Caring for Your Aging Parent

Reflections of the Heart
- A Journey Through Love Addiction

The Tapestry of Grief
- A Journey Through Loss

Navigating Divorce
- A Path Toward Transformation

Bridging the Relationship Void
- From Loneliness to Connection

The Sensitive Soul
- The Hidden Power of Your Empathy

Nature's Wisdom

- Awakening Consciousness Through Natural Connection

Pet Ownership
- Connecting with Our Companions & Discovering Ourselves

Embracing Aging
- A Journey of Self-Discovery

Transcending Guilt
- A Journey of Self-Discovery and Personal Transformation

Transcending Stress & Anxiety
- Finding Empowerment in Life's Challenges

Unlocking Your Financial Potential
- Reframing Your Money-Mindset

On the Road
– Navigating Traffic & Your Inner World

The Art of Being Single
- A Guide to Self-Exploration, Empowerment, &Fulfillment

Through the Lens of Estrangement
- Finding Yourself Amidst Family Challenges

Conscious Hearts
- On the Journey of Dating with Self-Respect

More to come...

Sign up for the newsletter to be notified of new books and receive exclusive offers!

www.wisdommanuals.com/newsletter

Books That Bring Awareness, Compassion & Insights Into Your Everyday Life
www.WisdomManuals.com

My professional website is: www.KimAronson.com
I offer intuitive readings to illuminate your path and provide clarity, personalized coaching sessions designed to empower you to reach your goals, and insightful teachings that will deepen your understanding of yourself and the world around you.

Wisdom Groups

Join today

Wisdom Groups For Contemplation & Conversation

A space for support, genuine reflection and deep discussion

M any of us feel a deep sense of disconnection in the face of life's challenges—from ourselves, others, and a meaningful purpose. Whether it's the grief of loss, the stress of everyday life, the pain of heartbreak, or the uncertainty of the future, these experiences often leave us feeling isolated, lost and longing for deeper understanding and connection.

Wisdom Groups are online Zoom groups inspired by this Wisdom Manuals book series. They are dedicated to bringing awareness, compassion and insights into everyday life, and offer a supportive environment to explore our shared struggles, reflect together, and transform pain into growth.

What to Expect in a Wisdom Group:

- **Weekly Gatherings:** Each session of 75 minutes begins with a topic or passage from one of the Wisdom Manuals books for contemplation, followed by group sharing and discussion.

- **Facilitated Conversations:** I'll guide our discussions to create a safe space for open sharing, reflection and mutual support. We'll explore awareness, consciousness and empathy as sources of strength to integrate wisdom into our everyday lives.

- **Planting Seeds Together:** Through shared reflections, we'll grow as a community by turning emotional pain into opportunities for self-discovery and deeper connection.

The inspiration for the Wisdom Manuals book series comes from my lifelong journey of questioning: Why are we here? How do we find meaning in our struggles? What can we learn from the difficult moments in life? Through creativity, personal experiences and spiritual exploration, I've discovered just how much wisdom can be embodied in our daily lives when we connect with others and face our challenges with an open heart.

Is This Group for You?

If you're feeling:

- Disconnected from yourself or others, yearning for a deeper connection
- Overwhelmed by everyday life
- Stuck in stress, anxiety or grief, needing a way forward
- Lonely or uncertain about your path in life, seeking a sense of meaning and belonging
- Curious about how to turn life's challenges into empowering growth

opportunities

Then a Wisdom Group can offer you a community and tools for deeper self-awareness, connection and transformation.

Join us as we explore, reflect, and grow—one meaningful conversation at a time.

For more information or to join a Wisdom Group, visit: https://www.wisdommanuals.com/wisdom-groups

Introduction

F inancial troubles can feel like an anchor, weighing us down and limiting our potential. But what if those very struggles could be the key to unlocking a more fulfilling and prosperous life? This book invites you on a transformative journey—one that goes far beyond budgets and spreadsheets. Here, we'll explore the hidden depths of your relationship with money, uncovering the beliefs, patterns, and untapped strengths that shape your financial reality.

Through ancient wisdom, psychological insights, and practical exercises, you'll learn to confront the fears and limiting beliefs holding you back and transform financial challenges into opportunities for profound personal growth. This is not just another finance self-help book. It's a roadmap to becoming more conscious, self-aware, and aligned with your authentic self. As you progress through these pages, you'll gain the tools to not only improve your financial situation but create a life of greater meaning, purpose, and abundance.

Are you ready to embark on this adventure? To see your financial struggles not as obstacles but as gateways to a more empowered version of yourself? Let's begin the journey to unlocking your true financial potential.

Chapter One

Ego Exploration

In the realm of personal finance, our ego plays a crucial role in shaping our attitudes, beliefs, and behaviors in relation to money. By becoming more conscious of how our ego influences our financial decisions, we can gain valuable insights into our spending habits, saving patterns, and overall financial well-being. As we delve into our ego's impact on our financial mindset, we open doors to possible transformation, empowering ourselves to make more conscious choices and cultivate a more balanced approach to our financial lives.

A Tale of Confrontation

In a bustling kingdom there lived a merchant named Elias who had grown wealthy but ignorant and arrogant. His ego, a magnificent suit of armor, shielded him from the struggles of those around him. One day, when a sudden recession hit, Elias lost everything. In despair, he wandered to the Mountains of Reflection, where he encountered a wise hermit. The hermit revealed that Elias's armor blinded him to the realities of life and the connections he could foster with others. As Elias began to shed his ego-driven armor piece by piece, he felt vulnerable and learned to be empathetic. He soon became a beloved figure who helped rebuild his community, piece by piece, just as he did his authentic self.

Reflection

This myth illustrates how the ego can act as a barrier, preventing us from seeing the truth of our circumstances and the needs of others. By embracing vulnerability, we can forge deeper connections with others—and ourselves—and become more conscious of our actions and their impacts.

Exercises

1. Financial Identity Reflection

The financial identity reflection exercise helps us uncover deep-seated beliefs and attitudes about money that are tied to our ego's understanding of finance. By exploring our financial identity, we can gain insight into how our self-perception influences our financial decisions and behaviors.

Find a quiet, comfortable space where you can reflect without interruption. Grab a pen and paper or open a document on your computer. Begin the exercise by completing the following statements related to your life and finances:

  1. "I am someone who ..."

  2. "When it comes to money, I ..."

  3. "My financial habits are ..."

4. "I view money as ..."

5. "My biggest financial fear is..."

6. "My relationship with money is ..."

7. "When I think about wealth, I feel ..."

8. "My financial goals are ..."

9. "My spending habits reflect ..."

10. "I believe I deserve ..."

As you write, allow your thoughts to flow freely without judgment. Be honest with yourself, even if some of your responses surprise you. After completing these statements, review what you've written. Look for patterns, recurring themes, or beliefs that stand out to you.

Now, take a step back and consider how these beliefs and attitudes might be influencing your financial decisions. Are there any limiting beliefs that you've identified? How might your ego be protecting or hindering you in your financial journey?

Next, challenge yourself to reframe any negative or limiting beliefs. For each one you identify, write an alternative, more empowering perspective. For example, you might reframe "I am someone who always struggles with money" as "I am someone who is learning to manage money effectively and grow my financial knowledge."

Reflect on how adopting these new perspectives might change your approach to financial challenges. Consider how your ego might evolve if you embraced these new beliefs.

Finally, set an intention to carry these insights forward. Choose one or two key realizations from this exercise and write down specific actions you can take to align your financial behaviors with your newly discovered, more empowering beliefs.

Example: Jill, a freelance designer, realized through this exercise that she viewed money as scarce and unstable, reflecting her irregular income. By reframing her limiting belief to "I am resourceful and capable of creating financial stability," she felt motivated to diversify her income streams and create a more robust financial plan.

2. Ego vs. Higher-Self Letter

This letter-writing exercise allows us to explore the dialogue between our ego's perspective on financial struggles and the wisdom of our higher self. By writing letters from these two viewpoints, we can gain insight into how our ego influences our financial decisions and receive compassionate guidance from our inner wisdom.

Find a quiet, comfortable space where you can write without interruption. Have two sheets of paper ready, or create two separate documents on your computer. Begin with writing the letter from your ego. At the top of the page, write "Dear Higher Self," and then allow your ego to express all its fears, frustrations, and concerns about your current financial situation.

Let your ego voice its worries, doubts, and any feelings of inadequacy or shame. Be raw and honest, allowing all emotions to surface.

Your ego might say things like ...

- "I'm terrified of never having enough money."

- "I feel like a failure because I can't manage my finances."

- "I'm ashamed of my debt and feel hopeless about ever paying it off."

- "I'm angry that others seem to have it all figured out while I struggle."

Write until you feel you've expressed everything your ego wants to say about your financial struggles. Sign the letter from "Your Ego."

Now, take a few deep breaths and center yourself. On the second sheet of paper or in a new document, write "Dear Ego," at the top; this is where you'll respond as your higher self. In this letter, tap into your inner wisdom, the part of you that is compassionate, understanding, and sees the bigger picture. From this perspective, offer comfort, advice, and insights to your ego.

Your higher self might say things like ...

- "I understand your fears, and it's okay to feel this way."

- "You're not alone in your struggles, and there is always hope for improvement."

- "Your worth is not determined by your financial situation."

- "Every challenge is an opportunity for growth and learning."

Offer specific guidance and encouragement to address the concerns raised by your ego. Suggest practical steps or mindset shifts that could help overcome financial challenges.

After completing both letters, read them through carefully. Notice the differences in tone, perspective, and energy between the two. Reflect on how the wisdom from your higher self can help soothe and guide your ego's fears and frustrations.

Consider what actions or changes you can implement based on the advice from your higher self. How can you bring more of this compassionate, wise perspective into your daily financial decisions?

Finally, write a short journal entry summarizing the key insights you've gained from this exercise and how you plan to apply them in your financial life. Keep these letters and your summary in a safe place, and return to them whenever you feel overwhelmed by financial stress.

Example: Edwin, struggling with credit card debt, wrote an ego letter expressing shame and hopelessness. His higher-self response emphasized his resilience and suggested a step-by-step debt repayment plan. This exercise helped Edwin approach his debt with a more balanced, solution-oriented mindset, reducing his anxiety and motivating him to take action.

3. Affirmation Practice

The affirmation practice exercise focuses on creating and using affirmations to challenge limiting beliefs about money that stem from our ego. By regularly repeating positive, empowering statements, we can reshape our financial mindset and foster a healthier self-image connected to financial wellness.

Find a quiet, comfortable space where you won't be disturbed. Begin by taking a few deep breaths to center yourself. Now, reflect on the limiting beliefs about money you've identified in previous exercises or that you're aware of in your daily life.

These might include thoughts like ...

- "I'll never be good with money."

- "Wanting more money is greedy."

- "I don't deserve financial abundance."

- "I'll always be in debt."

For each limiting belief you identify, create a positive affirmation that counters it. These affirmations should be personal "I" statements that are positive, in the present tense, specific, and emotionally engaging.

Here are a few examples of positive affirmations that counter each of the statements above, respectively:

- "I am becoming more financially savvy every day."

- "I can use my future wealth to create positive change."

- "I deserve financial abundance and welcome it into my life."

- "I am capable of managing my finances and becoming debt-free."

Set aside time each day to practice these new affirmations. In a quiet space, begin by taking a few deep breaths to center yourself, then read each affirmation out loud, slowly and with conviction. As you say each one, try to feel the truth of the statement in your body. Visualize yourself embodying this new belief.

Repeat each affirmation 3–5 times. If you encounter resistance or doubt, acknowledge it without judgment, then gently return your focus to the positive statement.

After you've gone through all your affirmations, take a moment to reflect on how you feel. Notice any shifts in your energy or mindset and reflect on how you can embody these affirmations as you go about your day.

Example: Harper, who always felt anxious about her finances, created the affirmation "I am calm and confident in managing my money." By repeating this daily, she noticed a gradual decrease in her financial anxiety and felt more empowered to create and stick to a budget, improving her overall financial health.

Altering Our Attitudes

American philosopher and psychologist William James once said, "The greatest discovery of my generation is that a human being can alter his life by altering his attitude." This quote suggests that by changing our attitude toward challenges, including financial struggles, we can transform our outcomes. In the context of the ego, embracing vulnerability and self-awareness can lead to personal growth and healthier relationships with money.

Chapter Two

The Masks that Make Us

Persona Awareness

I n the realm of financial struggles, our personas—the social masks we wear—play a crucial role in shaping our behaviors and decisions. These personas, often unconsciously adopted, can either hinder or support our financial well-being. By becoming more aware of these masks, we can gain valuable insights into our relationship with money and the societal pressures that influence our financial choices. This awareness allows us to make more conscious decisions, aligning our actions with our true values and goals.

A Tale of Revelation

Lina, a renowned actress, lived in a glamorous world, always playing the roles expected of her by society. When she faced financial ruin, her persona began to crack. Fearing the loss of her identity, she retreated to a hidden forest. There, she encountered a timid fox who shed its skin, revealing its true form beneath. Inspired, Lina removed her own mask and found solace in her authentic self. She learned to embrace simplicity and honesty, which led her to a new purpose: helping others in need.

Reflection

This story reveals that the persona, while sometimes necessary in society, can trap us in false or inauthentic identities. Stripping away these layers during times of financial hardship can lead to self-acceptance and a discovery of our true purpose.

Exercises

1. Walking Reflection

The walking reflection exercise encourages us to connect with nature while exploring our financial personas, providing a fresh perspective on our relationship with money.

Find a peaceful park or other natural setting for a solitary walk. As you begin your journey, focus on your breath and the sensation of your feet touching the ground. While you walk, allow your mind to wander to your various financial roles—perhaps as a provider, a saver, or a spender. Notice how these personas shift as you move through different areas of the park. Does the open field evoke feelings of financial freedom? Does a dense forest remind you of financial obstacles?

Pay attention to how your thoughts about money change based on your surroundings. Reflect on which of the personas feel most authentic to you and which feel imposed by external expectations. As you walk, consider how these personas influence your financial decisions in different aspects of your life—at home, at work, or in social settings. Notice any patterns or inconsistencies in how you approach money across these contexts.

Take mental notes of any insights or revelations that arise during your walk. Before concluding your journey, find a quiet spot to sit and reflect in your journal on what you've discovered about your financial personas. Consider how you might integrate this newfound awareness into your daily life to make more conscious financial choices.

Example: Sharon, a freelance graphic designer, took a mindful walk in her local botanical garden. As she strolled through the vibrant flower beds, she realized her "successful professional" persona often led her to overspend on unnecessary business expenses. In contrast, the serene Japanese garden reminded her of her desire for financial simplicity and stability. This awareness helped Sharon reconcile her conflicting financial behaviors and make more balanced decisions.

2. Narrative Collage

The narrative collage exercise helps us visualize and explore our financial journey through artistic expression, revealing insights about our personas' influences on our money mindset.

Gather a variety of magazines, newspapers, and personal photographs. Find a large piece of poster board or cardboard to serve as your canvas. To begin, flip through your gathered materials and select images, words, and colors that resonate with your financial experiences and the personas you've adopted throughout your life. Consider including representations of your childhood memories surrounding money, your current financial situation, and your future aspirations. Pay attention to the emotions these elements evoke.

Begin arranging these chosen pieces on your canvas, creating a visual narrative of your financial journey. Notice how different personas emerge in various stages of your story. Perhaps you see the "risk-taker" in your early career choices, or the "cautious saver" in your behavior as a child or teenager. Use colors and textures to represent the emotions associated with each persona. As you assemble your collage, reflect on how these personas have influenced your financial decisions and feelings about money. Are there any patterns or recurring themes? Are there any connections between seemingly unrelated elements of your collage?

Once you're finished, step back and observe your creation as a whole. What does it reveal about your relationship with money? Which personas dominate your financial narrative, and which are less prominent? Consider how you might balance these influences to create a more harmonious financial future. Display your collage in a visible location and revisit it regularly, using it as a tool for ongoing reflection and growth in your financial journey.

Example: Sebastian, a middle-aged teacher, created a financial narrative collage. He was surprised to see how prominently his "frugal provider" persona featured in the early years, represented by images of packed lunches and budget vacations. As the collage progressed, he noticed a shift towards a "status-seeker" persona, with luxury car ads and designer labels. This visual representation helped Sebastian understand his changing relationship with money and inspired him to find a balance between his competing financial identities.

3. Persona Sharing Group

The persona sharing group exercise fosters open dialogue about financial personas, encouraging mutual support and understanding among participants.

Organize a small group of 6–8 people who are comfortable discussing topics related to money and personal finance. Choose a quiet, private space where everyone can sit in a circle, fostering an open and welcoming environment. Begin the session by explaining the concept of financial personas and how they can influence our money decisions. Encourage participants to reflect on their own financial identities before sharing.

Start the sharing process by going around the circle and having each person (including yourself) describe one or two of their prominent financial personas. These might include "the provider," "the risk-taker," "the penny-pincher," or "the generous friend." Ask participants to explain how these personas manifest in their lives and the pressures they feel from each one. Encourage active listening from the group as each person shares.

After everyone has spoken, open the floor for discussion. Prompt participants to explore common themes or contrasts they noticed in the shared experiences. Encourage them to ask questions and offer support to one another. Guide the conversation towards understanding how societal expectations and personal histories shape these personas. Discuss strategies for becoming more aware of these personas in daily life and how to navigate conflicting financial identities.

Conclude the session by having each participant share one insight they gained from the group discussion and one action they plan to take to become more conscious of their financial personas. Encourage the group to continue supporting each other's journeys toward financial self-awareness beyond this session.

Example: A community center hosted a financial persona sharing group. During the session, Leticia, a young entrepreneur, realized her "ambitious go-getter" persona often clashed with her "security-seeking" side, causing financial stress. Hearing others' experiences helped Leticia feel less alone in her struggles and inspired her to find ways to honor both aspects of her financial identity. The group decided to meet monthly to continue supporting each other's financial growth.

Opportunities In Disguise

Pastor Charles R. Swindoll once said, "We are all faced with a series of great opportunities brilliantly disguised as impossible situations." This quote serves as a reminder that the challenges we face often provide hidden opportunities for growth. In relation to the persona, it encourages us to strip away social masks and embrace authenticity, realizing that our true self can navigate through difficult situations and emerge stronger than ever.

Chapter Three

The Hidden Self

Embracing Your Shadow

I n times of financial struggle, we often find ourselves grappling with emotions and behaviors that seem counterproductive or even self-sabotaging—parts of ourselves that we are embarrassed, ashamed, or in denial of. These hidden aspects of our personality, known as our Shadow, can play a significant role in shaping our relationship with money. By becoming aware of these hidden parts of ourselves, we can gain valuable insights into our financial patterns and make informed decisions. Embracing our Shadow allows us to confront our fears, insecurities, and limiting beliefs about money, paving the way for personal growth and financial well-being.

The Tale of the Lost Treasure

In a village overshadowed by its wealth, a young man named Tariq lived a life of blind ambition. One day, he stumbled upon a hidden cave containing the village's darkest secrets—greed, dishonesty, and envy. Initially terrified, Tariq soon realized these traits mirrored his own shadow. Rather than deny them, he embraced the uncomfortable truths and shared them with his community. This led to a transformative journey, one where Tariq and other villagers worked together to cultivate honesty and gratitude, embracing and reconciling their shadows for collective healing.

Reflection

The myth highlights that acknowledging our shadow, especially during financial struggles, can illuminate the hidden truths of our character. Embracing these aspects fosters growth and unity with others in the community facing similar challenges.

Exercises

1. Shadow Dialogue

The shadow dialogue exercise invites us to engage in a conversation with our financial shadow, allowing us to explore and understand the hidden aspects of our relationship with money.

Find a quiet, comfortable space where you won't be disturbed. Begin by taking a few deep breaths to center yourself. Imagine your financial shadow as a separate entity from yourself, giving it a form or shape in your mind. It could be a dark figure, an animal, or any other representation that feels right to you.

Now, initiate a dialogue with this shadow self. Ask it questions about your financial fears, insecurities, and habits. Allow the shadow to respond, giving voice to the thoughts and feelings you may have been suppressing.

As you engage in this conversation, remain open and curious. Ask your shadow why it behaves the way it does regarding money. What does it believe about wealth and abundance? Listen without judgment, allowing the shadow to express itself fully. You might ask questions like: "Why do you make me overspend when I'm stressed?" or "What are you afraid will happen if we save money? What are you afraid will happen if we spend?"

Pay attention to any resistance or discomfort you feel during this dialogue. These emotions often indicate areas where your shadow holds significant influence. Acknowledge these feelings and continue the conversation, exploring the root causes of your financial behaviors.

As the dialogue progresses, consider asking your shadow what it needs to feel secure about money. What can you do to address its concerns while still working towards your financial goals? This part of the conversation can lead to insights about how to integrate your shadow's needs with your conscious financial objectives.

Conclude the dialogue by thanking your shadow for its honesty and expressing your intention to work together toward your financial well-being. Take a moment to reflect on the conversation, noting any key insights or realizations that emerged.

Example: Lily, a freelance designer, engaged in a shadow dialogue about her tendency to undercharge clients. Her shadow revealed a deep-seated fear of rejection and unworthiness. By acknowledging these fears, Lily was able to develop strategies to value her work more appropriately, leading to improved financial stability and self-confidence in her business dealings.

2. Shadow Dream Journal

The shadow dream journal exercise encourages us to explore our subconscious mind through dream journaling, focusing specifically on dreams related to our financial fears and struggles.

Before going to sleep, set an intention to remember your dreams, particularly those related to money and finances. Keep a notebook and pen by your bedside. Upon waking, immediately write down any dreams you recall, no matter how fragmented or nonsensical they may seem. Pay special attention to dreams that evoke strong emotions or feature themes related to money, wealth, poverty, or financial transactions.

As you record your dreams, include as much detail as possible. Note the setting, characters, emotions, and any symbols or objects that stand out. Don't worry about writing in full sentences or interpreting the dream at this stage; focus on capturing the essence of the experience as vividly as you can.

After recording the dream, take some time to reflect on its potential meanings. Look for recurring themes, symbols, or emotions that appear in multiple dreams across several days.

Consider how the emotions and situations in your dreams might relate to your waking-life financial experiences. Are there any parallels between your dream scenarios and your current financial struggles? How do the characters in your dreams represent different aspects of yourself or your relationship with money?

Pay attention to any shadowy figures that appear in your dreams—characters that make you feel uncomfortable, threatened, or anxious. These figures often embody aspects of your financial shadow that you've been avoiding or repressing. Reflect on what these characters might be trying to tell you about your relationship with money.

As you continue this practice over time, you may start to notice patterns or shifts in your dream content. Perhaps your financial anxiety dreams become less frequent, or new symbols of abundance begin to appear. These changes can indicate progress in your journey of integrating your financial shadow.

Example: Henry consistently dreamed of drowning in coins. Through journaling, he realized this symbolized his fear of being overwhelmed by financial responsibilities. This awareness helped Henry develop a structured budget and seek financial advice, alleviating his anxiety and improving his money management skills.

3. Financial Tension Body Scan

The financial tension body scan exercise helps us connect with the physical manifestations of our financial stress, allowing us to identify and release tension related to money concerns.

Find a quiet, comfortable space where you won't be disturbed. Sit or lie down in a relaxed position, closing your eyes if it feels comfortable. Take a few deep breaths, allowing your body to settle into the present moment.

Begin by bringing your attention to your feet. Notice any sensations present—warmth, coolness, tingling, pressure. As you focus on your feet, consider if you're holding any tension related to your financial situation here. Perhaps you feel the weight of financial responsibility in your feet, or a restlessness to move forward financially.

Slowly move your attention up through your body, pausing at each area to notice sensations and any tension that might be related to your financial concerns. Pay particular attention to areas where you commonly hold stress, such as your legs, hips, stomach, chest, shoulders, neck, and face.

When you reach areas of significant tension, pause and explore the sensation more deeply. What does this tension feel like? Is it a tight knot, a heavy weight, a prickly sensation? Ask yourself what this physical sensation might be telling you about your relationship with money. For example, tightness in the chest might represent anxiety about financial instability, while tension in the shoulders could indicate the burden of financial responsibilities. Imagine your breath flowing directly into the tense area, bringing warmth and relaxation. As you exhale, visualize the tension dissolving and flowing out of your body.

Continue the body scan until you've reached the top of your head. Once complete, take a few moments to notice how your body feels as a whole. Are there areas that feel more relaxed now? Are there places where tension persists?

Conclude the exercise by setting an intention to carry this bodily awareness with you throughout your day. When you notice financial stress arising, return to your breath and scan your body, using this awareness as a tool to stay present and make conscious choices about your financial behavior.

Example: Molly discovered persistent tension in her jaw during the body scan. She realized this represented unexpressed anger about her financial situation. By acknowledging this emotion, Molly found the courage to negotiate a raise at work and set clearer boundaries with family members who often asked for money.

Acceptance Before Change

Psychologist Carl Jung once said, "We cannot change anything unless we accept it." This quote reflects the importance of acknowledging our shadow self. By accepting our hidden fears, anxieties, and insecurities, we can begin to understand and integrate them into our lives, ultimately paving the way for healing and personal transformation in our financial journey.

Chapter Four

Archetypes as Guides

A rchetypes can serve as powerful allies in our journey towards greater self-awareness and financial growth. Archetypes act as mirrors, reflecting aspects of ourselves we may have overlooked or forgotten, and as guides, illuminating paths to financial wisdom and empowerment. As you explore these timeless figures, you'll discover new perspectives on your relationship with money, enabling you to make more conscious choices and navigate financial challenges with greater clarity and purpose.

A Tale of Balance

A wise old sage named Zara traveled through three kingdoms, each ruled by an archetype: The Merchant, The Warrior, and The Healer. She observed their struggles with wealth and taught them about balance. The Merchant hoarded riches, the Warrior fought for dominance, and the Healer gave away too much. Together, after internalizing Zara's guidance the three kingdoms created a Council of Wisdom, combining their strengths while learning from each archetype. This newfound unity allowed them to face their financial hardships as one and rebuild their thriving kingdoms.

Reflection

This story shows that recognizing and integrating the different archetypes within us can lead to holistic development, especially when confronted with financial challenges. Each archetype offers lessons that can lead us to a balanced approach to wealth and resource management.

Exercises

1. Personal Archetype Inventory

The personal archetype inventory exercise helps us identify and explore the archetypes that influence our financial behaviors and decisions. By understanding these underlying patterns, we can gain valuable insights into our relationship with money.

Find a quiet, comfortable space where you can reflect without interruption. Begin by taking a few deep breaths to center yourself. Now, consider the various archetypes that resonate with you, particularly in relation to money; these might include the Hero, the Caregiver, the Rebel, the Sage, the Creator, or any others that come to mind. As you identify each archetype, write it down and spend some time reflecting on how it manifests in your financial life.

As you reflect, ask yourself the following:

> 1. How does this archetype influence my financial decisions?

> 2. What strengths does this archetype bring to my relationship with money?

3. What challenges or limitations might this archetype present?

4. How can I harness the positive aspects of this archetype to improve my financial situation?

Write a short description for each archetype, detailing its impact on your financial behaviors and decisions. Be honest and compassionate with yourself as you explore these patterns. For example, if you identify with the Hero archetype, you might write something like, "The Hero in me drives me to take risks and face financial challenges head-on. However, this archetype can sometimes lead me to take on too much responsibility or ignore my own needs in pursuit of a greater cause."

As you complete your inventory, look for patterns or themes that emerge. Are there archetypes that dominate your financial life? Are there others that you'd like to cultivate further? Consider how you can balance and integrate these different aspects of yourself to create a more holistic approach to your finances.

Example: Erin, a freelance designer, identified strongly with the Creator archetype in her financial life. She realized this drove her passion for innovative projects but also led to inconsistent income. By acknowledging this pattern, Erin began to balance her creative pursuits with more stable financial planning, leading to greater financial security without sacrificing her artistic vision.

2. Nature Archetype Walk

The nature archetype walk exercise encourages us to connect with archetypes through nature, offering a fresh perspective on our financial patterns and potential. By observing natural elements and relating them to archetypal qualities, we can gain new insights into our financial journey.

Choose a natural setting for your walk—a park, forest, beach, or any outdoor area where you can observe various natural elements. As you prepare for your walk, set an intention to be open and receptive to the archetypal symbols you might encounter. If possible, bring your journal and a pen or pencil.

Begin your walk at a slow, mindful pace. Take deep breaths and allow yourself to become fully present in the environment. As you move through the space, observe the natural elements around you. Look for objects, plants, or landscapes that catch your attention or evoke a particular feeling.

For each element that stands out to you, consider the following:

1. What archetype does this element remind you of?

2. What qualities or characteristics does it embody?

3. How might these qualities relate to your financial life?

For example, you might come across a sturdy oak tree and associate it with the Hero archetype. Reflect on its strength, endurance, and deep roots. How might these qualities apply to your financial journey? Perhaps they remind you of the importance of building a strong foundation or staying resilient in the face of financial challenges.

As you continue your walk, try to identify elements that represent different archetypes related to your financial life. You might see ...

- A flowing stream (the Trickster), representing adaptability and resourcefulness in managing money

- A nurturing bird's nest (the Caregiver), symbolizing the importance of financial security and providing for others

- A vibrant wildflower (the Creator), inspiring innovative approaches to generating income

After your walk, find a quiet spot to reflect on your experience. Write in your journal about what you observed in nature, and consider how the archetypes you encountered might offer new perspectives on your financial situation. How can you incorporate these qualities into your approach to money?

Example: During his nature walk, Willem noticed a small sapling growing through a crack in a rock. He associated this with the Explorer archetype, realizing that it symbolized his own resilience in finding opportunities amidst financial constraints. This insight inspired Willem to seek creative solutions to his current money challenges.

3. Archetype Dream Diary

The archetype dream diary exercise invites us to explore our subconscious mind through dreams, uncovering archetypal influences on our financial life. By recording and reflecting on dreams with financial themes, we can gain deeper insights into our relationship with money.

Begin by placing a notebook and pen next to your bed. Before going to sleep each night, set an intention to remember your dreams, particularly those related to money or financial situations. You speak aloud a positive affirmation, such as, "I will remember my dreams and pay attention to any financial themes or archetypal characters that appear."

Upon waking, immediately write down any dreams you remember, focusing on those with financial elements. Don't worry about making sense of them right away; simply record as many details as possible. Pay particular attention to any characters that appear in your dreams, as these may represent archetypal figures.

For each dream entry, include the following:

1. A brief description of the dream scenario

2. Any emotions you felt during the dream or as you woke up from it

3. Specific details about the dream's financial elements (money, valuables, transactions, etc.)

4. Descriptions of characters or figures that appeared in the dream

After recording the dream, take some time to reflect on its potential meanings, considering the following questions:

- What archetypal characters did I notice in the dream?

- How did these characters interact with financial elements in the dream?

- What roles did these archetypal figures play in the financial narrative?

- How might these dream scenarios relate to my waking financial life?

Look for patterns or recurring themes in your dreams over time. Do certain archetypes appear frequently? How do they influence the financial aspects of your dreams?

As you continue this practice, you may start to notice connections between your dream archetypes and your waking financial behaviors or attitudes. Use these insights to inform your conscious decisions and actions regarding money.

Example: Val dreamt of a wise old woman (the Sage archetype) showing her a hidden treasure in her backyard. Upon reflection, she realized this dream symbolized untapped financial potential within herself. This insight motivated Val to explore new skills and knowledge that could lead to better financial opportunities in her waking life.

Our Collective Memories

American psychiatrist Jean Shinoda Bolen once said, "Archetypes are the collective memories of mankind, and of the way we are." This quote highlights the idea that archetypes reside within our collective unconscious, influencing our thoughts and actions. By recognizing these universal patterns, we can gain valuable insights into our behaviors and motivations, ultimately guiding us toward a more balanced and prosperous financial life.

Chapter Five

Embracing Duality

The Masculine & Feminine

When facing financial challenges, it's common to lean heavily on one energy over the other. However, true financial wellness comes from harmonizing both masculine and feminine energies—which exist in all of us, regardless of our gender. The masculine energy can drive you to take decisive action, create structured plans, and pursue your financial goals with determination. Meanwhile, the feminine energy can allow for a more intuitive approach, helping you nurture your relationship with money, cultivate abundance mindsets, and find creative solutions to financial problems. By consciously working with both energies, you'll be better equipped to make conscious choices that align with your values and long-term goals.

A Journey to Wholeness

After a devastating flood, a village tucked away in a valley lost everything. Among the ruins, two figures emerged: Valen, the pragmatic warrior, and Lila, the nurturing caretaker. Initially, the two clashed in their approaches to rebuilding: Valen aimed for rapid construction and restoration, and Lila focusing on nurturing the villagers and fostering emotional healing. Eventually, the two figures realized that together, they could create sustainable solutions that would allow the land and those who inhabited it to not just survive, but thrive. By honoring both their masculine and feminine energies, they formed a community that celebrated resilience and creativity, emerging stronger than ever before.

Reflection

This tale emphasizes that integrating both masculine and feminine qualities can lead to a more comprehensive understanding of financial difficulties. This collaboration of energies fosters resilience and wholeness in overcoming adversity.

Exercises

1. Energy Collage

The energy collage exercise encourages us to explore the balance of masculine and feminine energies in our financial life through artistic expression. By creating this visual representation, we'll gain deeper insights into how these energies influence our financial decisions and attitudes.

Create an artwork that represents the interplay between masculine and feminine energies in your financial life. Begin by gathering a variety of materials that symbolize both masculine and feminine qualities. For masculine energy, consider using hard, structured materials like metal, wood, or sharp geometric shapes. For feminine energy, opt for softer, more fluid materials such as fabric, clay, or curved drawn lines.

Divide your canvas or workspace into two sections, one for each energy, leaving a small section in the center blank. In the masculine section, use bold colors and strong lines to represent assertiveness, logic, and action-oriented thinking in your financial life. You might depict symbols of goal setting, budgeting, or career advancement. In the feminine section, use softer colors and flowing forms to represent intuition, nurturing, and emotional aspects of your financial journey. This could include symbols of abundance, growth, or emotional well-being.

As you create, reflect on how these energies manifest in your financial decisions. Are there areas where you rely more heavily on one energy? How might integrating both energies lead to more balanced financial choices?

Once you've completed each side, focus on the central area you left blank: in this space, the two energies merge, representing the ideal balance of masculine and feminine in your financial life. Use a combination of materials and styles for this area to show how these energies can work together harmoniously.

After completing your artwork, take some time to journal about your experience. What did you learn about your financial approach? How can you apply these insights to achieve greater balance in your money management?

Display your artwork in a prominent place where you'll see it regularly. Let it serve as a reminder of the importance of balancing masculine and feminine energies in your financial life, inspiring you to make more conscious and balanced decisions moving forward.

Example: Aria, a journalist, created a collage representing her financial life. The masculine side showed structured budgets and career goals, while the feminine side depicted flowing abundance and intuitive in-

vestments. The center area blended both, revealing how balancing these energies could lead to more fulfilling financial decisions. This visual reminder helped Aria approach money matters with greater awareness and balance.

2. Opposite Energy Transformation

The opposite energy transformation exercise helps us identify and balance masculine and feminine energies in our financial decision-making process. By consciously exploring both aspects, we'll gain new perspectives on our financial challenges and opportunities.

Begin by creating two columns on a piece of paper, labeling one "Masculine" and the other "Feminine." Create a list of financial decisions you've made or situations you've experienced in the last few weeks, writing them either in the "Masculine" or "Feminine" column depending on the qualities it embodies and your intuitive sense of their energy.

In the masculine column, you might list actions like creating a strict budget, negotiating a salary increase, or making investment decisions based purely on data. In the feminine column, you might include experiences such as intuitive spending, nurturing your financial well-being through self-care, or making charitable donations based on an emotional connection to a cause.

Once you've compiled your lists, choose 2–3 items from each column that you feel are most significant to your current financial situation. For each of these items, write a short paragraph detailing how you typically approach this aspect of your finances.

Now, once you've done this, imagine fully embodying the opposite energy. How would your approach change? What new possibilities might emerge? Write down your thoughts and insights. For example, if "creating a budget" is in your masculine column, how might approaching it with feminine energy change the process? You might find yourself creating a more flexible, intuitive budget that aligns with your values and emotional needs, rather than focusing solely on rigid numbers. Conversely, if "intuitive spending" is in your feminine column, how might masculine energy enhance this practice? You could introduce a structured review process to analyze your intuitive purchases, ensuring they align with your long-term financial goals.

As you explore these alternative approaches, pay attention to any resistance or excitement you feel about each; these emotions can provide valuable insights into areas where you might benefit from greater balance.

Conclude the exercise by journaling about your experience. Reflect on how balancing masculine and feminine energies might lead to more conscious and effective financial management. Consider how you can incorporate this balanced approach into your broader financial strategy.

Example: Jackson, an accountant, typically approached investing with a purely masculine energy, focusing on data and logic. When he applied feminine energy to this process, he began considering his emotional connection to companies and their social impact. This balanced approach led to more fulfilling and successful investment decisions, aligning Jackson's portfolio with both his financial goals and personal values.

3. Balanced Energy Yoga

The balanced energy yoga practice is designed to help us physically experience and integrate masculine and feminine energies, providing an embodied understanding of balance that can be applied to our financial life.

Find a quiet, comfortable space for your practice. You'll need a yoga mat and comfortable clothing. If you have props like blocks or a strap, have them nearby. Set an intention to focus on balancing masculine and feminine energies in your financial life.

Begin the practice in a seated position, taking a few deep breaths to center yourself. As you inhale, imagine drawing in masculine energy: strong, assertive, and action-oriented qualities. As you exhale, envision feminine energy flowing through you: intuitive, nurturing, and receptive qualities.

Begin with a series of masculine energy poses. Move into Warrior I, holding the pose for five breaths. Feel the strength and stability in your legs, the power in your arms reaching skyward. This pose represents the assertiveness and goal-oriented nature of masculine energy in finances.

Transition to Warrior II, maintaining the strong stance but opening your chest and arms. This represents the balance of assertiveness (front leg) and receptivity (open arms) in financial decisions.

Move into a series of feminine-energy poses. Start with a seated forward fold, allowing your upper body to relax over your legs. This represents the ability to yield and be flexible in financial matters.

Transition to Child's Pose, focusing on the nurturing aspect of this position. Reflect on how you can nurture your financial well-being with compassion and self-care.

Next, flow through a series of poses that embody both energies. Begin with Sun Salutations, moving dynamically (masculine) while maintaining fluid, graceful movements (feminine). Include balance poses like Tree Pose, which require both strength (masculine) and flexibility (feminine). As you hold this pose, reflect on how you can bring both these qualities into your financial life.

Conclude the session with a few minutes in Savasana, allowing the experience to integrate fully. As you relax in this position, visualize the perfect balance of masculine and feminine energies in your approach to finances. After your practice, take some time to journal about your experience. How did it feel to embody these different energies? What insights did you gain about balancing masculine and feminine aspects in your financial life?

Commit to practicing this sequence regularly, perhaps weekly, as a physical reminder of the importance of balance in your financial approach. Over time, notice how this embodied understanding influences your financial decisions and overall relationship with money.

Example: Nora, a marketing executive, practiced this yoga sequence weekly. She found that the physical experience of balancing masculine and feminine energies translated clearly into her financial life. She became more assertive in negotiating contracts while also nurturing collaborative relationships with clients. This balanced approach led Norah to increased financial success and job satisfaction.

Reclaiming Earth's Energy

Environmental activist Vandana Shiva once said, "We need to reclaim the earth, the family, the community, and the personal attributes of integration, equality, harmony, and reciprocity." This quote reminds us of the crucial balance of masculine and feminine energies, emphasizing cooperation, harmony, and integration. In the context of financial struggle, Shiva encourages us to blend assertiveness with nurturing, leading to a more holistic approach to our financial lives that values both action and intuition.

Chapter Six

Harnessing Active Imagination

A ctive imagination is a powerful tool that can help you become more conscious and self-aware when dealing with financial struggles. This creative technique allows you to explore your inner world, uncovering hidden thoughts, feelings, and motivations related to money. By engaging in imaginative exercises, you can gain new insights into your financial behaviors, beliefs, and patterns. Through active imagination, you can tap into your subconscious mind, unlocking creative solutions to financial challenges and inspiring positive change in your financial life.

The Dream Weaver's Gift

In a land where dreams deeply influence reality, a young weaver named Adara struggled with her family's financial crisis. Seeking clarity, Adara entered a state of active imagination, where she met a spirit who guided her through the tapestry of her mind. Each thread represented her fears, hopes, and untapped potential. By weaving her dreams into her waking life, Adara transformed nightmares into patterns of opportunity, ultimately forging a new, prosperous path for her family.

Reflection

This narrative highlights the transformative power of active imagination. By confronting and integrating our dreams, we can explore creative solutions to financial struggles, gaining new perspectives on our situation.

Exercises

1. Imaginative Character Sketching

This exercise helps us visualize and understand different aspects of our financial life by creating characters that represent various financial roles or behaviors.

Find a quiet, comfortable space where you won't be disturbed. Begin by closing your eyes and taking a few deep breaths to center yourself. As you relax, imagine several characters emerging from your mind, each representing an aspect of your financial life. There might be a Saver, a Spender, an Investor, or a Worrier. Allow these characters to take physical shape; give them distinct personalities, appearances, and backgrounds that reflect the aspects of your financial story.

Now, open your eyes and begin to draw or paint these characters. Don't worry about artistic perfection; focus on capturing the essence of each being. As you create, pay attention to the details that emerge. What clothes are the characters wearing? What objects surround them? What facial expressions do they have?

For the Saver, you might draw a cautious figure clutching a piggy bank in a vault-like room. The Spender could be a carefree character surrounded by shopping bags in a bustling mall. The Investor might be depicted as a strategic chess player in a sleek office, while the Worrier could be huddled under a rain cloud made of dollar signs.

As you sketch, allow your intuition to guide you. What colors feel right for each character? What symbols or objects appear in their surroundings? These details can offer insights into your subconscious feelings about different financial behaviors.

Once you've finished your character sketches, take some time to reflect on what you've created. What do these characters reveal about your financial attitudes and behaviors? Are there any surprises or patterns you notice? Write down your observations and insights.

Now, imagine these characters interacting with each other. How do they communicate? Do they cooperate or conflict? This interaction can represent the different financial forces at play in your life.

Finally, consider how you might balance these characters to create a healthier financial narrative. Could the Saver teach the Spender some restraint? Could the Investor help the Worrier find more security? Use these insights to set intentions for your financial journey.

Example: Phoebe, struggling with overspending, drew her Spender as a vibrant butterfly in a garden of tempting flowers (representing her purchases). Her Saver appeared as a stern librarian in a quiet, orderly room. Reflecting on these images, Phoebe realized she needed to find balance between joy and restraint in her spending habits.

2. Nature Character Walk

The nature character walk exercise combines the grounding effects of nature with the imaginative power of character dialogue to explore our financial mindset.

Begin by finding a natural setting for your walk—a park, forest trail, or even a quiet, tree-lined street. As you start walking, take deep breaths and center yourself in the present moment. Feel the ground beneath your feet, the air on your skin, and observe the natural world around you.

As you walk, imagine that you begin to encounter the characters from the previous exercise who represent different aspects of your financial life. These characters might emerge from behind trees, appear on the path ahead, or even manifest as the natural elements around you. As you approach each character, engage them in a conversation. Ask them about their philosophy on money, their fears, and their advice for you. Listen carefully to their responses, which are coming from a part of your own psyche.

As you engage with the characters you come across, consider the following questions:

- What does this character have to say about the role of money in life?

- What is this character fearful of regarding money?

- What can you learn from this character's approach to finances?

As you conclude your walk, take a moment to stand still and integrate the insights you've gained. How can you incorporate the wisdom of each character into your financial life? What balance do you need to strike?

Finally, express gratitude to each character and to nature for the insights provided. As you return from your walk, carry these lessons with you and set an intention to apply them to your real-world financial decisions.

Example: During his nature walk, Leo encountered his Investor as a beaver building a dam. This character emphasized the importance of consistent, incremental efforts in building financial security. Leo realized he needed to make small, regular investments rather than waiting for a large windfall to start planning for his future.

3. Financial Intentions Ceremony

The financial intentions ceremony helps us honor our financial achievements and set intentions for future growth through a meaningful ritual.

Begin by creating a sacred space for your ceremony. Find a quiet, comfortable space where you won't be disturbed. Gather and arrange personal items from around your home that can represent your financial journey and achievements. These might include a piggy bank symbolizing savings, a vision board depicting financial goals you've reached or strive toward, or objects representing specific skills you've developed.

Light a candle to signify the start of your ceremony. Take a few deep breaths, centering yourself in the present moment. Reflect on your financial journey, acknowledging both the challenges you've faced and the progress you've made.

Now, write down on small pieces of paper the financial goals you've achieved or the aspects of your financial shadow you've successfully confronted. These could range from paying off a debt to overcoming a fear of investing. Hold each paper, fully acknowledging the effort and growth it represents.

One by one, burn these papers safely in a fireproof container (or tear them up if burning them isn't feasible). As each paper burns, say out loud, "I honor this achievement and release it, making space for new growth."

Next, take a new sheet of paper and write down your intentions for future financial growth. Be specific but also open to unexpected opportunities. These intentions might include developing new financial habits, seeking education in a particular area of finance, or working towards a significant financial goal.

Hold this paper to your heart, imagining the energy of your intentions flowing into your being. Then, fold the paper and place it in a special container or envelope that you'll keep in a meaningful place.

To close the ceremony, speak words of gratitude for your financial journey thus far and your excitement for the path ahead. You might say something like, "I am grateful for the lessons I've learned and the growth I've experienced. I move forward with confidence, wisdom, and openness to abundance in all its forms."

Extinguish the candle, signifying the end of the ceremony. Keep your intention paper in a place where you'll see it regularly, serving as a reminder of your commitment to financial growth and self-awareness.

Example: Claire conducted a ceremony to mark paying off her student loans. She burned a paper representing her debt, feeling a weight lift off her shoulders. Claire then wrote intentions for building an emergency fund and investing in her skills.

Let Your Imagination Fly

American writer Laura Ingalls Wilder once said, "Imagination is the highest kite one can fly." This quote underscores the importance of active imagination as a means of creative exploration and problem solving. By tapping into our imagination, we can uncover innovative solutions to financial challenges and transform our relationship with money into one of possibility and growth.

Chapter Seven

Alchemical Transformation

I n the realm of personal growth, alchemy serves as a powerful metaphor for the transformative journey we undertake when facing financial struggles. Just as ancient alchemists sought to turn base metals into gold, we, too, can transmute our financial challenges into opportunities for self-discovery and growth. By embracing the principles of alchemy, we can shift our perspective on financial difficulties, viewing them not as insurmountable obstacles but as catalysts for personal evolution. This approach empowers us to recognize the hidden potential within our struggles, transforming them into stepping stones toward greater wisdom and financial well-being.

The Alchemist's Journey

Long ago, a once-prosperous city fell into despair following financial collapse. An alchemist named Penelope sought the fabled Philosopher's Stone to create limitless gold. Instead, she discovered that true alchemy lay not in wealth—but in transforming her mindset. By changing leaden thoughts of scarcity into golden beliefs of abundance, the city flourished again as its citizens learned to value community, shared resources, and sustainability over material gain.

Reflection

This myth illustrates the concept of psychological transformation through alchemy. It encourages us to shift our mindset from scarcity to abundance, allowing us to thrive in financial adversity through community and shared values.

Exercises

1. Transformation Journal

The transformation journal exercise encourages us to document our financial challenges and reflect on how they can serve as catalysts for personal growth and transformation.

Maintain a dedicated journal for recording your financial experiences, challenges, and insights. Each day, take 10–15 minutes to write about any financial situations you encounter, both struggles and successes. Describe the events in detail, including your thoughts, emotions, and actions in response to these situations.

As you document these experiences, reflect on how each challenge can be viewed as an opportunity for personal transformation.

Ask yourself questions like the following:

- What lessons can I learn from this situation?

- How can this difficulty lead to a new understanding or insight about myself or my relationship with money?

- What strengths or skills am I developing as I navigate this challenge?

Consider how your responses to financial situations have changed over time. Are you noticing patterns in your behavior or thought processes? Are there areas where you've grown or developed new perspectives?

Regularly review your journal entries to identify recurring themes or areas of progress. Look for instances where you've successfully transformed a challenge into an opportunity for growth. Celebrate these moments of transformation and consider how you can apply the lessons learned to future financial situations.

Example: Maurice started her transformation journal during a period of unemployment. She documented her daily struggles with job hunting and budgeting but also reflected on the skills she was developing, like resilience and creativity. Over time, Maurice noticed a shift in her entries from fear-based reactions to more proactive problem solving, marking her personal growth through financial adversity.

2. Limiting-Belief Alchemy

The limiting-belief alchemy exercise helps us identify and transform limiting beliefs about finances into empowering statements, shifting our mindset toward abundance and possibility.

Find a quiet, comfortable space where you won't be disturbed. Begin by settling into a comfortable position, closing your eyes, and taking a few deep breaths to center yourself. Now, in your journal or on a piece of paper, create two columns. In the left column, list all the limiting beliefs you hold about money and your financial situation. These might include thoughts like "I'll never be good with money,"

"Rich people are greedy," or "I don't deserve financial abundance."

Take your time with this step, allowing yourself to uncover beliefs that may have been operating beneath the surface of your conscious awareness. Be honest with yourself, writing down even those beliefs that may feel uncomfortable or embarrassing to acknowledge.

Once you've listed your limiting beliefs, turn your attention to the right column. For each limiting belief, craft a transformed statement that reframes it positively. For example, "I'll never be good with money" might become "I am learning to manage my finances effectively and growing more confident each day."

As you create these transformed statements, pay attention to how they feel. Do they resonate with you? Do they feel authentic and achievable? If not, adjust the wording until you find a statement that feels both positive and believable.

After you've transformed all your limiting beliefs, take some time to reflect on this process. How does it feel to see your beliefs side by side with their transformed counterparts? Notice any shifts in your energy or perspective as you contemplate these new, empowering statements.

Practice reading your transformed statements aloud each day. As you do so, allow yourself to fully embody the energy and mindset of these new beliefs. Visualize yourself living as if these statements were already true for you.

Throughout your day, catch yourself when old limiting beliefs arise. In those moments, consciously choose to replace the limiting belief with its transformed counterpart. Over time, this practice will help rewire your thought patterns and shift your overall mindset about money.

Example: Dovid, a small business owner, realized his belief "I'm not cut out for financial success" was holding him back. During this exercise, he transformed it to "I have the skills and determination to achieve financial success." This shift inspired Dovid to seek mentorship and take calculated risks, leading to significant growth in his business and personal finances.

3. Alchemical Storytelling

The alchemical storytelling creative exercise invites us to explore financial transformation through the lens of storytelling, using the metaphor of alchemy to gain new insights and perspectives on our financial life.

Find a quiet, comfortable space where you can let your imagination flow freely. Take a few deep breaths to center yourself and clear your mind. Now, imagine yourself as an alchemist embarking on a journey to transform base metals (your financial struggles) into gold (financial abundance and wisdom).

In your journal, begin writing a short story or poem about this alchemical journey, allowing your narrative to unfold naturally. Don't worry about perfect grammar or structure; focus on the flow of ideas and emotions. Describe the alchemist's journey in detail: What challenges do they face? What tools or resources do they discover along the way? Who do they meet, and what lessons do these encounters teach them?

As you write, consider the symbolic meaning behind the elements of your story. The base metals might represent specific financial challenges you're facing, while the process of transformation could symbolize the steps you're taking to overcome these challenges. The gold at the end of the journey might represent not just financial abundance but also the wisdom and personal growth gained through the process.

Explore the emotions your alchemist experiences throughout their journey. How do they handle setbacks? What moments of insight or breakthrough do they have? How does their perspective on wealth and abundance change as they progress?

Don't rush to a conclusion. Allow your story to develop at its own pace, reflecting the often-gradual nature of personal and financial transformation. When you feel your story has reached its natural end, take some time to reflect on what you've written, noting any themes, symbols, or insights that stand out to you. How does the alchemist's journey mirror your own financial journey? What lessons from the story can you apply to your own life?

Consider sharing your story with a trusted friend or financial advisor. Sometimes, others can offer perspectives or interpretations we might miss on our own. Discuss how the metaphors in your story relate to real-life financial strategies or personal growth opportunities.

Example: Bronwyn wrote a story about an alchemist transforming rust (debt) into gold (financial freedom). In her tale, the alchemist learned patience, sought wisdom from unexpected sources, and discovered inner strength. This process helped Bronwyn reframe her approach to paying off student loans, inspiring her to seek financial education and celebrate small victories along the way.

Alchemy as Self-Transformation

Author Anne Baring once wrote, "The great alchemical process works in the depths of our being and brings about self-transformation." This quote highlights the transformational journey we undertake when facing personal struggles, including financial ones. Just as alchemy aims to turn base metals into gold, we can transmute our financial challenges into opportunities for profound self-discovery and growth.

Chapter Eight

Awakening Through Synchronicity

I n the realm of personal growth and financial well-being, synchronicity emerges as a powerful tool for cultivating self-awareness. Recognizing and embracing synchronistic events can offer profound insights and guidance, serving as signposts that direct our attention to hidden patterns, overlooked opportunities, and deeper truths about our relationship with money and abundance. This awareness allows us to perceive our financial challenges from a broader perspective, unveiling the lessons and growth opportunities embedded within them. As we become more adept at recognizing these synchronistic moments, we cultivate a sense of flow and alignment with the universe, fostering trust in the unfolding of our financial journey.

The Weaving of Fate

In a small village, Lucia, a seamstress, found herself in dire financial straits. As she worked tirelessly day in and day out, she noticed the strange coincidences occurring around her—people visiting at exactly the right time, materials appearing unexpectedly. Intrigued, Lucia began to trust in the wisdom of these synchronicities, leading her to new opportunities and collaborations that revitalized her business. As she continued to work, the village prospered as connections deepened, and all villagers began to acknowledge the magic of their intertwined destinies.

Reflection

This story illustrates how synchronicity can guide us during financial hardships. By being open to the seemingly coincidental events in our lives, we can uncover paths to overcoming challenges and rediscovering purpose.

Exercises

1. Thematic Reflection

The thematic reflection exercise helps us identify recurring themes in our financial life and explore how they may correlate with synchronicities we've experienced.

Create a series of worksheets to track and analyze patterns in your financial behaviors and experiences. Start by designing a spending pattern worksheet. List your expenses for the past month, categorizing them by type (e.g., necessities, luxuries, impulse buys). Next to each item, note any emotions or thoughts associated with the purchase.

Next, create a saving pattern worksheet. Record your saving habits over the past few months. Include successful savings, missed opportunities, and any obstacles you encountered. Reflect on the circumstances surrounding these patterns.

Develop an income flow worksheet. Document your sources of income, including unexpected windfalls or financial gifts. Note any patterns or fluctuations in your income streams.

On each worksheet, include a section for synchronicities. Record any meaningful coincidences related to each financial aspect. For example, did you unexpectedly receive money when you most needed it? Did a conversation about budgeting lead to a job opportunity?

After completing these worksheets, create a synthesis page. Here, look for overarching themes across your financial life. Are there recurring patterns in your spending when you're stressed? Do your saving habits correlate with certain life events?

Next, examine how these patterns relate to the synchronicities you've noted. Do you notice any connections between your financial behaviors and meaningful coincidences? For instance, do you tend to experience positive synchronicities when you're more mindful of your spending?

Reflect on what these patterns and synchronicities might be revealing about your relationship with money. Are they highlighting areas for growth or change? Are they affirming positive financial habits?

Use these insights to set intentions for your financial future. How can you align your actions with the positive patterns and synchronicities you've observed? What changes can you make to address challenging patterns?

Revisit and update these worksheets regularly, perhaps monthly or quarterly. Over time, you may notice larger patterns emerging, providing deeper insights into your financial journey and personal growth.

Example: Charlie created financial pattern worksheets and noticed that he often received unexpected income after volunteering. This synchronicity made him realize the connection between generosity and abundance in his life. Charlie began allocating a portion of his budget to charitable giving, which unexpectedly led to new networking opportunities and a more fulfilling career path.

2. Envisioning Ceremony

The envisioning ceremony guides us through creating a personal ceremony to visualize our financial goals while recognizing past synchronicities, fostering trust in the universe's flow.

Begin by setting aside uninterrupted time in a quiet, comfortable space. Gather materials such as candles, incense, crystals, and any other objects that hold personal significance for you. These items will help create a sacred atmosphere for your ceremony.

Begin your ceremony by cleansing your space. You might choose to sage the area, ring a bell, or simply take a few deep breaths to clear the energy. As you do this, set an intention to open yourself to guidance and insight regarding your financial journey.

Light a candle to symbolize illumination and clarity in your financial life. Take a moment to center yourself, focusing on your breath and allowing any tension to melt away.

Now, reflect on past synchronicities related to your finances. Recall moments when unexpected opportunities arose, when you received timely advice, or when seemingly random events led to positive financial outcomes. Write these experiences down, expressing gratitude for each one.

With these synchronicities in mind, turn your attention to your current financial goals. Visualize each goal as vividly as possible. See yourself achieving financial stability, abundance, or whatever represents success to you. As you hold these images, remain open to any insights or messages that may arise.

On a piece of paper, write down intentions that relate to trusting in the flow of the universe. These might include statements like "I trust that the right opportunities will come my way" or "I am open to receiving abundance in unexpected forms."

Create a symbolic action to represent your commitment to these intentions. This could be tying a knot in a piece of string, planting a seed, or placing a stone in water. As you perform this action, re-affirm your trust in the universe's guidance.

Take a moment to listen. Sit in silence, allowing any final insights or feelings to surface. Pay attention to any symbols, words, or images that come to mind.

Close your ceremony by expressing gratitude for the guidance and insights you've received. Extinguish the candle, symbolizing the completion of this visioning process.

After the ceremony, journal about your experience. Note any particularly powerful moments, insights, or emotions that arose during the process. In the days and weeks following your ceremony, remain alert to synchronicities that may relate to your financial goals and intentions. When you notice them, acknowledge them with gratitude, seeing them as confirmations of your alignment with the universe's flow .

Consider repeating this ceremony periodically, perhaps monthly or with the new moon, to reinforce your intentions and maintain your connection with the synchronicities guiding your financial journey.

Example: During his visioning ceremony, Marcus recalled a synchronicity where a book on investing literally fell off a shelf in front of him. This memory inspired him to set an intention to remain open to unexpected financial wisdom. A week later, he stumbled upon a free workshop on sustainable investing, which aligned perfectly with his values and financial goals.

3. Guided Dream Visualization

The guided dream visualization exercise helps us tap into our subconscious mind to receive insights about synchronicity in our financial life through dream work.

Before beginning this exercise, create a comfortable and relaxing environment in your bedroom. Ensure you have your journal and a pen near your bed to capture your dreams upon waking.

As you prepare for sleep, take a few deep breaths to center yourself. Set a clear intention to be open to receiving messages through your dreams related to synchronicity in your financial life. You might say to yourself, "I am open to receiving guidance about my financial journey through my dreams tonight."

As you lay down and close your eyes, visualize yourself in a peaceful, natural setting—perhaps a serene forest or a tranquil beach. In this place, imagine encountering a wise guide who represents your inner wisdom. Ask this guide to show you symbols or messages related to synchronicity in your financial life.

As you drift off to sleep, hold this intention lightly in your mind. Don't try to force anything; simply remain open to whatever may come. Upon waking, whether in the middle of the night or in the morning, immediately record any dreams, fragments, or impressions you recall. Don't worry about making sense of them at this point; simply capture as much detail as possible.

Once you've recorded your dreams, take some time to reflect on them. Look for symbols, themes, or emotions that might relate to your financial life. Pay particular attention to any elements that seem unusual or stand out strongly. Consider how these dream elements might connect to synchronicities you've experienced in your waking life. Are there any parallels or insights that emerge?

Throughout your day, remain alert to any events, conversations, or occurrences that seem to echo elements from your dreams. These could be potential synchronicities guiding you towards greater financial awareness.

Keep a dream journal dedicated to this practice. Over time, you may start to notice patterns or recurring themes that offer deeper insights into your financial journey.

Example: After setting an intention to receive financial guidance through her dreams, Mira dreamt of a golden key opening multiple doors. The next day, she received an unexpected invitation to a network-

ing event. This synchronicity led her to attend, where she met a mentor who provided crucial advice for advancing her career and improving her financial situation.

An Ever-Present Reality

Swiss psychologist and psychotherapist C. G. Jung once said, "Synchronicity is an ever-present reality for those who have eyes to see." Jung emphasizes the importance of being aware and open to the meaningful coincidences in our lives. In relation to financial challenges, he encourages us to recognize how synchronicities can reveal insights and connections that guide us toward better choices and opportunities.

Chapter Nine

Nurturing Your Authentic Self

A Path to Greater Consciousness

W hen facing financial hardship, it's easy to lose sight of your true self. However, by connecting with your authentic core, you can navigate these challenges with greater awareness and purpose. The concept of The Self offers a powerful framework for personal growth, enabling you to tap into your inner wisdom and align your financial decisions with your deepest values. As you become more self-aware, you'll discover new perspectives on your financial situation, uncovering opportunities for growth and transformation.

The Quest for Wholeness

In ancient times, a warrior named Kai set out on a quest to find a legendary gem said to grant the seeker their heart's desires. Starving and desolate, he faced trials that stripped him of material wealth and forced him to confront his insecurities and aspirations. After a long and arduous journey, Kai realized that the true gem was within him—the Self, encompassing both his struggles and aspirations. Returning home, he helped others connect with their inner gems, fostering a community grounded in self-awareness and inner richness.

Reflection

This myth illustrates the importance of the search for the Self and how financial struggles can lead us to a deeper understanding of our identity. By exploring our inner world, we can tap into our true potential, paving the way for resilience and growth.

Exercises

1. Financial-Self Vision

The financial-self vision exercise helps us envision our ideal financial self, aligning our goals with our authentic values and aspirations.

Find a quiet, comfortable space where you won't be disturbed. Take a few moments to close your eyes and take several deep breaths, grounding yourself in the present moment. Now, with your eyes closed, picture your ideal financial self—the version of you that has a healthy, balanced relationship with money. This self embodies confidence, wisdom, and clarity when it comes to financial matters.

When you feel ready, open your eyes and begin writing a letter from this perspective to your present self. Begin by addressing yourself with compassion and understanding. Describe how you, as your ideal financial self, approach money matters. What mindset do you embody? How do you make financial decisions? Share your financial goals and the steps you're taking to achieve them. Offer guidance on overcoming current challenges, drawing from the wisdom and experience of your ideal self.

Reflect on the values that guide your financial choices. How do these align with your authentic self? Describe the feeling of security and freedom that comes from this aligned approach to finances. Share insights on balancing material needs with spiritual or personal growth.

Offer words of encouragement to your present self. Acknowledge the journey ahead and express confidence in your ability to grow and transform. Remind yourself of your inner strength and the resources available to you.

As you conclude the letter, invite your present self to embody these qualities and perspectives. Sign off with a powerful affirmation or statement that encapsulates your vision for your financial self.

After writing, read the letter aloud to yourself. Feel the emotions and energy behind the words. Keep this letter as a touchstone, returning to it when you need guidance or motivation in your financial journey.

Example:

Dear Present Self,

I am you, but with a clear vision of our financial future. We approach money with calm confidence, aligning our spending with our values of sustainability and community. We've learned to balance saving for the future with enjoying the present. Remember, every financial decision is an opportunity for growth. Trust in your ability to make wise choices.

With love and faith in you,

Your Future Self

2. Self-Portrait of Financial Identity

This self-portrait exercise uses artistic expression to reveal hidden aspects of our relationship with money and self-worth.

Gather art materials that resonate with you—colored pencils, markers, paints, magazines for collage, or any other medium. Create a quiet, contemplative environment free from distractions. Begin with five minutes of centered breathing to connect with your inner wisdom.

Now, close your eyes and visualize your relationship with money. What colors represent your financial emotions? What symbols naturally emerge? Do you see landscapes, patterns, abstract shapes? Notice how your body feels as these images arise. Let your intuition guide your artistic choices without judgment or criticism.

Begin creating your self-portrait, allowing it to evolve organically. Express different aspects of your financial identity through visual elements—perhaps spirals for growth, bridges for transition, or mountains for challenges. Consider using warm colors for areas where you feel confident about money, and cooler tones for aspects that feel uncertain. Add symbols representing your hopes, fears, and dreams about financial abundance.

As you work, pay attention to ...

- The size and placement of different elements

- The types of lines you use (sharp, flowing, broken, continuous)

- The balance between light and dark areas

- Symbols that appear unexpectedly

- Areas you feel drawn to or resist completing

Take time to layer your creation, adding depth and texture. You might include words, numbers, or phrases that hold significance in your financial story. Consider how past experiences with money influence your choices of color and form. Notice if certain areas of the portrait feel more authentic or challenging to express.

When you're finished, sit with your creation. Write in your journal about what you observe, what surprises you, and what insights have emerged about your self-worth and your relationship with money.

Example: Zackary drew himself surrounded by dark clouds (representing debt) with golden rays (symbolizing potential) breaking through. At the bottom, he added deep roots reaching into rich soil, revealing his unconscious belief in his fundamental resourcefulness. This visual representation helped Zackary recognize his resilience and capacity for transformation despite financial struggles.

3. Peer Support Group

The peer support group exercise helps us create a supportive community for sharing financial experiences and fostering collective growth.

Reach out to friends, colleagues, or community members who might be interested in forming a financial support group. Aim for a small group of 4–8 people to ensure intimate, meaningful discussions. Establish a regular meeting schedule (e.g., weekly, bi-weekly, monthly) and choose a comfortable, private location or opt for virtual meetings if more convenient.

At the first session, set clear guidelines for participation; emphasize confidentiality, respect, and non-judgment. Create a safe space where members feel comfortable sharing their authentic selves in relation to financial matters.

Structure each meeting with a clear format. Start with a brief check-in where each member shares their current financial state of mind. Follow with a main discussion topic, which could rotate among members or be decided collectively.

Encourage members to share their financial stories, both struggles and successes. Focus on how these experiences relate to each person's authentic self. Discuss questions like, How do your financial habits align with your values? What financial decisions have brought you closer to or further from your true self?

Incorporate exercises or activities that promote self-awareness and growth. This could include sharing financial goals, discussing books on money mindset, or practicing visualization techniques for financial success.

Foster an environment of mutual support and accountability. Encourage members to set personal financial goals and report back on their progress. Celebrate successes, no matter how small, and offer support during challenges.

Regularly reflect on how the group is impacting each member's financial consciousness and self-awareness. Are people feeling more aligned with their authentic selves? Are they making financial decisions with greater clarity and purpose?

As the group evolves, be open to adjusting the format or focus to meet the changing needs of its members. Remember, the goal is collective growth through mutual support and shared experiences.

Example: Maria started a financial support group with five friends. In their meetings, they shared personal stories about money, from childhood memories to current challenges. One member, Tom, realized his overspending stemmed from a need for validation. The group's support helped him more closely align his spending with his true values, leading to more fulfilling financial choices and a stronger sense of self.

Asserting Oneself

French philosopher Albert Camus once said, "To know oneself, one should assert oneself." This quote speaks to the necessity of self-awareness and expression in understanding our true identity. In the context of financial struggles, reclaiming our authentic selves empowers us to make choices that are aligned with our core values, ultimately leading to a healthier relationship with money.

Chapter Ten

What's Next?

C ongratulations on completing your journey through *Unlocking Your Financial Potential*. You've taken an important step in your journey toward financial freedom by exploring the complexities of the self and your relationship with money. Each chapter has provided you with unique insights and practical exercises designed to empower you to glean insights from your financial endeavors and nurture your own well-being. As you reflect on your experiences, consider the following action steps to integrate your newfound knowledge into your everyday life:

Reflect on Your Growth:

Take some time to revisit the sections of this book that resonated with you the most. Reflect on what you've learned about yourself, your financial goals, and your overall relationship with money. Create a routine that includes journaling, meditating, or both to foster deep reflection and capture your insights and emotions. Engage in this self-reflection regularly; it will help you maintain awareness as you navigate future challenges.

Set Intentions for the Future:

As you move forward, take a moment to envision your desired future. What aspirations do you have for the coming weeks, months, and years related to wealth and finance? Write down these intentions, and revisit them regularly, allowing them to guide your actions and decisions. Setting clear goals for your personal evolution as you continue your journey will help you remain aligned with your authentic self.

Engage in Mindfulness:

Maintain a mindful approach to your daily life. Practice being present and aware of your surroundings, your thoughts, and feelings. Regular practices such as meditation, journaling, or mindful observation of nature, can help you remain centered and present. These practices will support you in staying connected to your emotions without becoming overwhelmed.

Integrate Learnings into Your Daily Life:

Make a conscious effort to incorporate the lessons and values you've learned here into your daily life throughout your financial endeavors and beyond. Create and commit to a regular routine that incorporates these practices and allow them to evolve as you continue to process your emotions and experiences.

Practice Self-Care & -Compassion:

Remember to always be gentle and compassionate with yourself as you journey through financial struggles. Healing is not linear: growth takes time, and it's okay to experience setbacks. Practice kindness towards yourself in these moments, recognizing your strengths and celebrating your journey. Develop a daily practice that nurtures you, whether through self-care routines, hobbies that bring you joy, or spending time with supportive friends and family. Your well-being, both mental and physical, is essential for you to navigate your emotions in a balanced, holistic way.

Honor Your Progress:

Just by completing this book, you have made significant strides. Celebrate the growth you've achieved throughout this process. Acknowledge both the small victories and the significant transformations. This gratitude will reinforce your journey and empower you as you step into your next chapter.

Connect With Your Community:

Engaging with community can provide encouragement, understanding, and opportunities for shared growth. Connect with others who are on a similar journey and share your experiences, insights, and challenges. Seek support from loved ones or find a forum or workshop where you can engage in discussions about money and finances as you continue to heal and grow. Remember, you're not alone on this journey. Your story has the potential to inspire and uplift, creating a ripple effect of awareness and understanding.

As you conclude this chapter and step into the next phase of your journey, remember that your financial journey is not just about saving and spending —it's an ongoing opportunity for fulfillment and transformation. By applying the principles you've learned and the tools you've developed throughout this book, you are equipped to navigate the challenges ahead with resilience and compassion. Embrace new experiences with an open heart and remain attuned to the transformative power of this process. Your journey forward is bright, filled with endless possibilities for personal growth and a richer understanding of life's unfolding narrative.

The Wisdom Manuals Series

Books That Bring Awareness, Compassion & Insights Into Your Everyday Life

This book is part of my Wisdom Manuals series. This book series was inspired first and foremost by a wish to incorporate spiritual wisdom into our daily lives. We are here to learn—to become conscious and awake throughout our lives. I truly believe that the way to find happiness and purpose in life is to be aware of all aspects of ourselves.

The Wisdom Manual series focuses on two things:

Helping us become more conscious—which helps us make good decisions, build self-awareness, engage in social interaction, solve problems, be more creative and productive, and be happier and more fulfilled

Integrating wisdom and consciousness into what we already do daily

Since I was very young, I've had questions about life. Why are we here? What are we supposed to learn? What is this thing called "wisdom," anyway?

Over the years, I have read many books about these very topics. But still, I have struggled with connecting with a single spiritual practice or disciplines. In many ways, creativity has become my spiritual go-to; I have found that the best wisdom can be found in what you experience in your body and daily life.

As a foundation for this series, I've used Jung's theory of the individuation process. Carl Gustav Jung (1875–1961) was a Swiss psychiatrist and psychoanalyst who founded analytical psychology.

Jung believed that our minds have two main parts: the part we're aware of (our conscious) and the part we're unaware of (our unconscious). He thought that to grow as people, we must understand and bring together these different parts of ourselves.

Jung came up with an idea called the "individuation process"—a journey we take to become complete and well balanced. Here's what this journey involves:

Getting to know different parts of ourselves, including how we act in public, our hidden thoughts and feelings, and typical behavior patterns all humans share

Understanding our dreams and using our imagination to learn more about our unconscious mind

Finding a balance between different sides of our personality, like the masculine and feminine qualities we all have

Becoming more "whole" and understanding ourselves better, including facing our inner struggles and accepting the good and bad parts of who we are

Not to be "perfect," but rather to become more truly ourselves, understanding and accepting our differences.

—◦◈◦—

In the following pages, I offer short explanations of the concepts I use in my books:

Ego

Your ego is your sense of self—how you think of yourself and how you actin the world. It's the part of your mind that helps you make decisions, interact with others, and create your identity. Your ego helps you understand who you are and how you fit into your environment.

Persona

Your persona is the mask you wear when you are around other people—the version of yourself that you show to the world. This can include how you behave at work, with friends, or even in family settings. While the persona helps you fit in and connect with others, it can sometimes hide your true feelings or thoughts.

Shadow

Your shadow represents the parts of yourself that you try to keep hidden. This could include feelings, traits, or thoughts that you don't want to acknowledge—such as anger, fear, or insecurity. Everyone has a shadow, and understanding it can help you grow. Recognizing your shadow helps you acceptall parts of yourself—both the good and the b ad.

Archetypes

Archetypes are universal symbols or themes found in stories, myths, and dreams. They represent different aspects of human experience. Examples include the Hero, the Caregiver, and the Rebel. These archetypes can guide you and shape your behavior by showing you the roles you might play in your life and relationships.

Masculine/Feminine Qualities

Everyone has both masculine and feminine qualities, regardless of gender or sex. Masculine traits might include strength and assertiveness, while feminine traits might include nurturing and compassion. Understanding these qualities helps you find balance within yourself. Acknowledging both sides can create a healthier view of relationships and personal growth.

Active Imagination

Active imagination is a technique that involves using your imagination to explore your thoughts and feelings. It often includes visualizing conversations with parts of yourself or characters from your dreams. This practice helps you tap into your inner thoughts and feelings, leading to better self-understanding.

Alchemy

Alchemy (the process of turning metals into gold) related to the self is about transformation. In Jung's work, it symbolizes turning negative feelings(like fear or pain) into positive growth (like wisdom or strength). The process of alchemy represents your journey to change and heal by learning from your experiences.

Synchronicity

Synchronicity refers to the meaningful coincidences that happen in your life. These events may be connected even if they don't appear to have a cause-and-effect relationship. Recognizing these moments can help you understand your path and feel more connected to the world around you.

Self

The self is the complete picture of who you are. It includes both your conscious and unconscious parts. Finding a balance between these aspects can lead to personal fulfillment and understanding. Embracing your true self means recognizing all parts of you—your strengths, weaknesses, desires, and fears.

These concepts can help you explore yourself more deeply and understand how you interact with others and the world. By reflecting on them, you can gain insights that support your personal growth and relationships.

The Creator

About Kim Aronson

I grew up in Copenhagen, Denmark, in the 1960s and '70s. As a child, I wasn't the best student. I could never sit still, and I think I would have probably been diagnosed with ADHD. I also didn't know at the time that I was dyslexic—no one did. I hated writing, and I couldn't make sense of any of the words I saw on the page. But if someone handed me some markers and glue, I was in heaven! I loved being creative, and this creativity provided me with a much-needed outlet for my other academic frustrations.

Throughout my life, I've always been an early adopter of technology. When I sat in front of a computer at an event in a Library in Copenhagen in 1995, where they were "showing off" the internet, I was *mesmerized*. After this, my first project using technology was creating customized icons that I sold at the local Mac store. A bit later, I started creating animations using Macromedia Director. Those moments became my first experiences of merging my creativity and technology. It allowed me to express myself without limits.

I created many online services in the late '90s and early 2000s, including a social network site in Denmark called Mandala. I also created a search site for spiritual seekers called ZenSearch, among many others.

However, the one that stuck around and became very successful was my online dating site, Soulmate, which I founded before creating a few other US-based dating sites over the next few years.

Although you've indeed just finished one of my books, I'm still not much of a writer. I love expressing myself and have always had many ideas and insights to share, but writing has been hard for me. This is why I've learned, over the last few years, all about the wonders of AI and LLM (Large Language Models). I have discovered how these programs can help me express my thoughts, feelings, and the wisdom I've accumulated over many years. It helps me communicate what's important to me and what I feel would be essential and helpful for others. As such, this book series has, to an extended degree, been created with the help of AI.

I hope you find the insights and exercises in this book and the rest of the series useful and inspiring. Please contact me with any thoughts, ideas, or wisdom to share. I would enjoy connecting.

www.WisdomManuals.com

My professional website is: www.KimAronson.com
I offer intuitive readings to illuminate your path and provide clarity, personalized coaching sessions designed to empower you to reach your goals, and insightful teachings that will deepen your understanding of yourself and the world around you.

www.ingramcontent.com/pod-product-compliance
Lightning Source LLC
Chambersburg PA
CBHW052328220526
45472CB00001B/321